A Project Report on

COMMON DATABASE INTERFACE

Submitted to the partial fulfillment of the requirements for the award of the
degree of
Bachelor of Technology
in
Computer Science and Engineering

Submitted by:

SAJAD AHMAD RATHER (CS-10-45)
UMER LONE (CS-10-57)
MUNEER KHAN (CS-10-38)

Under the Guidance of:

Mr. SHOWKAT AHMAD
Assistant Professor
Department of Computer Science and Engineering

SESSION 2010-2014

DEPARTMENT OF COMPUTER SCIENCE AND ENGINEERING

ISLAMIC UNIVERSITY OF SCIENCE AND TECHNOLOGY

i

BONAFIDE CERTIFICATE

Certified that project work entitled "*Common Database Interface*" is the bonafide work of Sajad Ahmad Rather (CS-10-45),Umer Lone (CS-10-57),Muneer Khan (CS-10-38) who carried out the research under my supervision. Certified further, that to the best of my knowledge the work reporting herein does not form part of any other project report or dissertation on the basis of which a degree or award was conferred on an earlier occasion on this or any other candidate.

....
(Signature)

Mr. SHOWKAT AHMAD
Supervisor
Assistant Professor
IUST, Awantipora

....
(Signature)

Prof.(Dr.) A.G. Lone
Head of Department
IUST, Awantipora

Internal Examiner

External Examiner

ACKNOWLEDGEMENT

I feel an immense amount of pleasure in completing and submitting this project report on *"Common Database Interface"* as fulfillment for the award of the Degree of B.Tech in Computer Science and Engineering. The satisfaction and euphoria that accompany the successful completion of any project would be incomplete without a mention of people who made it possible and whose constant guidance and encouragement crown all the efforts.

First, I would like to express my sincere gratitude to my advisor, **Mr. Showkat Ahmad** for his invaluable guidance and cooperation throughout the work. His constant encouragement and vision enabled me to take this new endeavor to the success path.

I feel compelled to articulate my thankfulness to **Mr. Sajad Sir**, **Mr. Asif Sir,** Project Coordinator, whose constant motivation and support made me enthusiastic throughout the work.

Also, I extend my sincere regards and thanks to **Prof.(Dr.) A.G. Lone**, Head of Department, Computer Science and Engineering, IUST, Awantipora, Pulwama for his support and encouragement throughout the work and for providing the suitable environment to carry out the work.

I would like to express my hearty gratitude to **Dr. Trag Sir**, Vice Chancellor IUST, Awantipora, Pulwama for his support and encouragement throughout the work and for providing the suitable environment to carry out the work.

In the last but not least I am indebted to all the teaching and non-teaching staff members of our college for helping me directly or indirectly by all means throughout the course of my study and project work.

DECLARATION

We, Sajad **Ahmad Rather (CS-10-45), Umer Lone (CS-10-57), Muneer Khan (CS-10-38** hereby declare that the work which is being presented in the dissertation "*Common Database Interface*" is the record of authentic work carried out by me under the supervision of **Mr. Showkat Ahmad** in the Department of Computer Science and Engineering, IUST, Awantipora, Pulwama and submitted in the fulfillment for the award of the degree of **Bachelor of Technology** in Computer Science and Engineering. This work has not been submitted to any other University or Institute for the award of any Degree/Diploma.

Sajad Ahmad Rather, Umer Lone, Muneer Khan

CONTENTS Page No.

ABSTRACT

Today Computer-based information technologies have been extensively used to help many organizations, private companies, and academic and education institutions manage their processes and information systems hereby become their nervous centre. The explosion of massive data sets created by businesses, science and governments necessitates intelligent and more powerful computing paradigms so that users can benefit from this data. Therefore most new-generation database applications demand intelligent information management to enhance efficient interactions between database and the users. So, our aim is to develop an enhanced engine that will help us to provide an environment where an expert user as well as a non-expert user will be able to write and execute the database queries with ease and efficiency and without the proper knowledge of SQL (Structured Query Language), which is the basic language to interact with the database server. The aim of our project is to make a non-expert user to access the database without the prior knowledge of SQL and to provide an easy interface to expert user also, so that it will also get an easy way to interact with database and doesn't need to remember the syntax of commonly used queries to interact with the database. This enhanced engine provides access to users based on the credential User-Id and password. When access is granted, the user can use this enhanced engine to manipulate its database.

This enhanced engine allows common users to only retrieve the information from database using a natural language (English) and to the database administrator all the interfaces are available which will help it to manage, modify and update its database with ease.

CHAPTER - 1

INTRODUCTION

1.1 Project Overview

1.2 Problem Definition

PROJECT OVERVIEW:

Databases are gaining prime importance in a huge variety of application areas employing private and public information systems. A general information management system that is capable of managing several kinds of data, stored in the database is known as Database Management System (DBMS). The DBMS grants support for logical views of data that are separate from the physical views, i.e. how the data is actually stored in the database. By permitting applications to define, access, and update data through a Data Definition Language (DDL) and Data Manipulation Language (DML) combined into a declarative query language such as the relational query language SQL the separation is accomplished.

Structured Query Language (SQL) is an ANSI standard for accessing and manipulating the information stored in relational databases. It is comprehensively employed in industry and is supported by major database management systems (DBMS). Most of the languages used for manipulating relational database systems are based on the norms of SQL. They work on the basis of Boolean interpretation of the queries: a logical expression is the only accepted selection criterion and the response always encompasses only these tuples for what the expression results in a true value. But some user requirements may not be answered

2

explicitly by a classic querying system. It is due to the fact that the requirements' characteristics cannot be expressed by regular query languages. Many novel-generation database applications stipulate intelligent information management necessitating efficient interactions between the users and database. In recent times, there is a rising demands for non-expert users to query relational databases in a more natural language encompassing linguistic variables and terms, instead of operating on the values of the attributes. Intelligent database systems, a promising approach, enhance the users in performing flexible querying in databases. One of the essential characteristic of intelligent database management systems is the ability to provide automated support to users to maintain the semantic correctness of data in compliance to the integrity constraints. These integrity constraints are a vital means to characterize the well- formedness and semantics of the information stored in databases.

Intelligent Information Processing is defined as a study on fundamental theory and advanced technology of intelligence and knowledge for information processing. Knowledge-based systems have qualified to offer services in a well-founded ontological framework and there are a number of tools available to support intelligent knowledge management. The techniques of Artificial Intelligence can serve as effective tools in this context. The intelligent systems have a wide range of applications ranging from surfing through the Internet and data-mining, interpreting Internet-derived material, the human Web interface, remote condition monitoring and many other regions.

Thus, we have taken all these considerations into the mind and we have designed an intelligent interface "Enhanced Engine For Robust Database Querying" which will process the non-expert user's query (which is in natural language "English") and will transform it into the SQL query, which will be easily understood by the DBMS, which then executes it and produces the desired output to the user.

For the expert user (who has the knowledge of SQL), we have developed some interfaces in this enhanced engine which provides the expert user with some ready-made components, helping it to easily choose a particular query and execute it, thus the expert user doesn't have to remember the syntax of each and every SQL query.

Thus, our project has a basic home-page which will provide the introduction to the user about the system and its working and functionality and provides the access to all the interfaces designed. The different interfaces include: natural language processing interface which is responsible for processing the natural language query and retrieve the desired result; another interface is that of the expert user which provides it will all the commonly used SQL queries and displays the different databases and tables and also the data-types of different attributes of tables; another interface is the schema description interface which presents the schema of all the tables in the database and provides an easy way to modify the structure of any tables; another interface helps to create the user of database by just providing the details about the user.

Thus by this way our project has provided an easy environment to the user for interacting with the database with all functionalities and requirements and with our project even a lay-man can easy extract any information from the database which it was not able to achieve with the application programs developed by the programmers for a user.

1.1 <u>PROBLEM DEFINITION:</u>

This is first and most important phase of the SDLC in which System Analyst carries out preliminary investigation of the current system with the intention of locating the problems of current system. After finding out the problem we suggest the list of solutions which will enable the organization to overcome the above problem.

Today each and every organization needs database for storing information, and we have analyzed that there can be expert or non-expert users of database. For non-expert users of database (who doesn't have got the prior knowledge of SQL), the designers provide an easy interface by which they can extract only limited information from the database, depending on the fields provided by the designer, but if the user wants to extract some other fields of database, it is not able to do so because of the limited fields provided by the software designer. To overcome this problem we have designed the intelligent engine which will help the non-expert user to interact with the database with a natural language (English), and then the user will be able to extract any field's data with an ease. Also it is evident that most of the people are related with database, even a lay-man and to interact with the database it is not necessary that the user will have the knowledge about the SQL which will help it to interact with database, for this reason programmers provide application programs to the user with which it can retrieve limited information from the database, but with our enhanced system user can extract limitless information which is present in the database. Thus making it easy for everyone who uses database to extract information from it without prior knowledge of SQL or other additional information.

Also for the expert user, the problem is to remember the syntax of different queries, which is a cumbersome process, to overcome this problem we have designed some interfaces by which an expert user not only can extract information from the database, but also can modify the structure and data of database. Also another problem is that user does not remember the names of different databases and tables, to operate on them it must extract names of different databases and tables, to overcome this problem our enhanced engine automatically provides the list of all databases and their tables.

Thus by this way we will be able to overcome the problems associated with the expert as well as the non-expert user, and provide an easy interface for both to interact with database and achieve the desired result easily, efficiently and quickly.

PROPOSED SYSTEM

2.1 OVERVIEW:

With advances and in-deep applications of computer technologies, in particular, the extensive applications of Web technology in various areas, databases have become the repositories of large volumes of data.. It is known that databases respond only to standard SQL queries and it is highly impossible for a common person to be well versed in SQL querying. Moreover they may be unaware of the database structures namely table formats, their fields with corresponding types, primary keys and more. On account of these we design an intelligent layer which accepts common user's imperative sentences as input and converts them into standard SQL queries to retrieve data from relational databases based on knowledge base. The primary advantage of the system is that it conceals the inherent complexity involved in information retrieval based on unqualified user queries.

We propose to develop an intelligent layer which can be incorporated with the existing database system, which is responsible for the intelligent information processing and performing flexible queries. The user queries are given in a more conversing language using linguistic variables and terms. The intelligent layer designed in our scheme processes the unqualified user query and constructs a Standard SQL query from it.

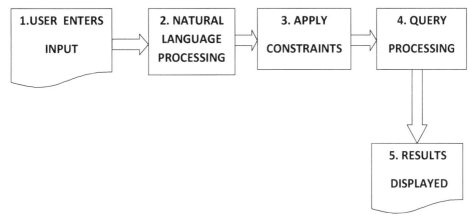

"Overview Diagram Of The Proposed System"

2.2 SYSTEM FEATURES:

1. Visual Interface:

The interface developed is graphical that makes it easy to handle for users and easy to use by a non-expert user also to interact with different databases.

2. Inbuilt Query Generator:

By this feature, we can generate queries graphically and don't need to write as command line, we just have to click a button and the query will be generated by itself.

3. Natural Language Query:

This feature provides an easy interface to non-expert user where the user can type the query in natural language (English) and can fetch the desired information from the database.

4. Schema Description:

Our project also provides an easy way to access the schema description of database and provides an easy way to modify it with just few clicks.

5. Database Lists:

Our enhanced system also provides a list of databases and their corresponding tables in the system, by which user can easy keep an eye on different databases and is easily known about the number and names of different databases in its system.

6. Web Based:

This feature avoid following drawbacks of windows based application:

1) A hectic burden of installation of windows based software on different systems.

2) Web based needs only browsing at any place.

3) It is fast and easy accessible.

4) Web pages can contain pictures, buttons and even links to sound files, in addition to text, thus allowing multimedia applications.

2.3 FACILITIES PROVIDED:

As the proposed system was developed to overcome the problems which were in the current system. The following feature was taken into the consideration in the development process of this web-based Enhanced Engine:

- Natural Language processing.
- Visual interface.
- Editable data-grid-view.
- Access all types of database.
- Easy way to create a new user.
- Graphical user interface.
- Inbuilt Query generator.
- Easy way to delete an existing user.
- Retrieve query wizard
- Schema Description.

With all these things this enhanced engine will provide a robust way of querying a database and provides those functionalities to the system by which it can be also operated by a lay-man and can retrieve any kind of information from its database. Also these facilities of the system provide additional features to the traditional system and hence increasing the efficiency of the system.

2.4 NATURAL LANGUAGE PROCESSING (NLP):

It is a field of computer science, artificial intelligence, and linguistics concerned with the interactions between computers and human (natural) languages. As such, NLP is related to the area of human–computer interaction. Many challenges in NLP involve natural language understanding, that is, enabling computers to derive meaning from human or natural language input, and others involve natural language generation. NLP using machine learning Modern NLP algorithms are based on machine learning, especially statistical machine learning. The paradigm of machine learning is different from that of most prior attempts at language processing. Prior implementations of language-processing tasks typically involved the direct hand coding of large sets of rules. The machine-learning paradigm calls instead for using general learning algorithms — often, although not always, grounded in statistical inference — to automatically learn such rules through the analysis of large corpora of typical real-world examples.

Many different classes of machine learning algorithms have been applied to NLP tasks. These algorithms take as input a large set of "features" that are generated from the input data. Some of the earliest-used algorithms, such as decision trees, produced systems of hard if-then rules similar to the systems of hand-written rules that were then common. Increasingly, however, research has focused on statistical models, which make soft, probabilistic decisions based on attaching real-valued weights to each input feature. Such models have the advantage that they can express the relative certainty of many different possible answers rather than only one, producing more reliable results when such a model is included as a component of a larger system.

Systems based on machine-learning algorithms have many advantages over hand-produced rules: The learning procedures used during machine learning automatically focus on the most common cases, whereas when writing rules by hand it is often not obvious at all where the effort should be directed. Automatic learning procedures can make use of statistical inference algorithms to produce models that are robust to unfamiliar input (e.g. containing words or structures that have not been seen before) and to erroneous input (e.g. with misspelled words or words accidentally omitted). Generally, handling such input gracefully with hand-written rules — or more generally, creating systems of hand- written rules that make soft decisions — is extremely difficult, error-prone and time- consuming. Systems based on automatically learning the rules can be made more accurate simply by supplying more input data. However, systems based on hand-written rules can only be made more accurate by increasing the complexity of the rules, which is a much more difficult task. In particular, there is a limit to the complexity of systems based on hand- crafted rules, beyond which the systems become more and more unmanageable. However, creating more data to input to machine learning systems simply requires a corresponding increase in the number of man- hours worked, generally without significant increases in the complexity of the annotation process.

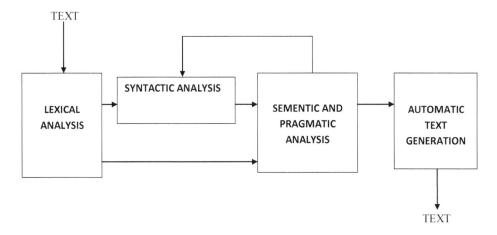

"COMMON PROCESSES IN NLP"

2.4.1 <u>Major tasks in NLP</u>

Automatic summarization

Produce a readable summary of a chunk of text. Often used to provide summaries of text of a known type, such as articles in the financial section of a newspaper. Co-reference resolution Given a sentence or larger chunk of text, determine which words ("mentions") refer to the same objects ("entities"). Anaphora resolution is a specific example of this task, and is specifically concerned with matching up pronouns with the nouns or names that they refer to. The more general task of co-reference resolution also includes identifying so-called "bridging relationships" involving referring expressions. For example, in a sentence such as "He entered John's house through the front door", "the front door" is a referring expression and the bridging relationship to be identified is the fact that the door being referred to is the front door of John's house (rather than of some other structure that might also be referred to).

Discourse analysis

This rubric includes a number of related tasks. One task is identifying the discourse structure of connected text, i.e. the nature of the discourse relationships between sentences (e.g. elaboration, explanation, contrast). Another possible task is recognizing and classifying the speech acts in a chunk of text (e.g. yes-no question, content question, statement, assertion, etc.).

Machine translation

Automatically translate text from one human language to another. This is one of the most difficult problems, and is a member of a class of problems colloquially termed " AI-complete ", i.e. requiring all of the different types of knowledge that humans possess (grammar, semantics, facts about the real world, etc.) in order to solve properly.

Morphological segmentation

Separate words into individual morphemes and identify the class of the morphemes. The difficulty of this task depends greatly on the complexity of the morphology (i.e. the structure of words) of the language being considered. English has fairly simple morphology, especially inflectional morphology, and thus it is often possible to ignore this task entirely and simply model all possible forms of a word (e.g. "open, opens, opened, and opening") as separate words. In languages such as Turkish, however, such an approach is not possible, as each dictionary entry has thousands of possible word forms.

Named entity recognition (NER)

Given a stream of text, determine which items in the text map to proper names, such as people or places, and what the type of each such name is (e.g. person, location, organization). Note that, although capitalization can aid in recognizing named entities in languages such as English, this information cannot aid in determining the type of named entity, and in any case is often inaccurate or insufficient. For example, the first word of a sentence is also capitalized, and named entities often span several words, only some of which are capitalized. Furthermore, many other languages in non-Western scripts (e.g. Chinese or Arabic) do not have any capitalization at all, and even languages with capitalization may not consistently use it to distinguish names. For example, German capitalizes all nouns, regardless of whether they refer to names, and French and Spanish do not capitalize names that serve as adjectives .

Natural language generation

Convert information from computer databases into readable human language. Natural language understanding Convert chunks of text into more formal representations such as first-order logic structures that are easier for computer programs to manipulate. Natural language understanding involves the identification of the intended semantic from the multiple possible semantics which can be derived from a natural language expression which usually takes the form of organized notations of natural languages concepts. Introduction and creation of language meta-model and ontology are efficient however empirical solutions. An explicit formalization of natural languages semantics without confusions with implicit assumptions such as closed world assumption (CWA) vs. open world assumption, or subjective Yes/No vs. objective True/False is expected for the construction of a basis of semantics formalization.

Optical character recognition (OCR)

Given an image representing printed text, determine the corresponding text. Part-of-speech tagging given a sentence, determine the part of speech for each word. Many words, especially common ones, can serve as multiple parts of speech. For example, "book" can be a noun ("the book on the table") or verb ("to book a flight"); "set" can be a noun, verb or adjective; and "out" can be any of at least five different parts of speech. Some languages have more such ambiguity than others. Languages with little inflectional morphology, such as English are particularly prone to such ambiguity. Chinese is prone to such ambiguity because it is a tonal language during verbalization. Such inflection is not readily conveyed via the entities employed within the orthography to convey intended meaning. Parsing determine the parse tree (grammatical analysis) of a given sentence. The grammar for natural languages is ambiguous and typical sentences have multiple possible analyses. In fact, perhaps surprisingly, for a typical sentence there may be thousands of potential parses (most of which will seem completely nonsensical to a human).

Question answering

Given a human-language question, determine its answer. Typical questions have a specific right answer (such as "What is the capital of Canada?"), but sometimes open-ended questions are also considered (such as "What is the meaning of life?"). Relationship extraction given a chunk of text, identify the relationships among named entities (e.g. who is the wife of whom). Sentence breaking (also known as sentence boundary disambiguation) given a chunk of text, find the sentence boundaries. Sentence boundaries are often marked by periods or other punctuation marks, but these same characters can serve other purposes (e.g. marking abbreviations).

Sentiment analysis

Extract subjective information usually from a set of documents, often using online reviews to determine "polarity" about specific objects. It is especially useful for identifying trends of public opinion in the social media, for the purpose of marketing.

Speech recognition

Given a sound clip of a person or people speaking, determine the textual representation of the speech. This is the opposite of text to speech and is one of the extremely difficult problems colloquially termed "AI-complete" (see above). In natural speech there are hardly any pauses between successive words, and thus speech segmentation is a necessary subtask of speech recognition (see below). Note also that in most spoken languages, the sounds representing successive letters blend into each other in a process termed co-articulation, so the conversion of the analog signal to discrete characters can be a very difficult process.

Speech segmentation

Given a sound clip of a person or people speaking, separate it into words. A subtask of speech recognition and typically grouped with it.

Topic segmentation and recognition

Given a chunk of text, separate it into segments each of which is devoted to a topic, and identify the topic of the segment. Speech processing is also a part of it this covers speech recognition, text-to- speech and related tasks.

Word segmentation

Separate a chunk of continuous text into separate words. For a language like English, this is fairly trivial, since words are usually separated by spaces. However, some written languages like Chinese , Japanese and Thai do not mark word boundaries in such a fashion, and in those languages text segmentation is a significant task requiring knowledge of the vocabulary and morphology of words in the language. Word sense disambiguation Many words have more than one meaning ; we have to select the meaning which makes the most sense in context. For this problem, we are typically given a list of words and associated word senses, e.g. from a dictionary or from an online resource such as Word Net . In some cases, sets of related tasks are grouped into subfields of NLP that are often considered separately from NLP as a whole. Examples include:

Information retrieval (IR)

This is concerned with storing, searching and retrieving information. It is a separate field within computer science (closer to databases), but IR relies on some NLP methods (for example, stemming). Some current research and applications seek to bridge the gap between IR and NLP.

Information extraction (IE)

This is concerned in general with the extraction of semantic information from text. This covers tasks such as named entity recognition, Co-reference resolution, relationship extraction, etc.

Query Evaluator:

It executes low-level instruction generated by compiler. Thus, the query-execution engine takes a query-evaluation plan, executes that plan, and returns the answers to the query. Annotated expression specifying detailed evaluation strategy is called an evaluation-plan. Query Optimization is amongst all equivalent evaluation plans choose the one with lowest cost. A query evaluation plan (or simply plan) consists of an extended relational algebra tree, with additional annotations at each node indicating: The access methods to use for each table; the implementation method. When the query involves several operators, sometimes the result of one is pipelined into the next. In this case, no temporary relation is written to disk (materialized). The result is fed to the next operator as soon as it is available. When the input table to a unary operator is pipelined into it, we say it is applied on-the-fly

Buffer Manager:

It keeps all those files which were recently used by the engine, so that they could be used again. Thus, it increases the efficiency and the speed of the query engine. So the main job of buffer manager is to manage the buffer memory and replace those files from it which are not likely to be used frequently. The buffer manager reads disk pages into a main memory page as needed. The collection of main memory pages (called frames) used by the buffer manager for this purpose is called the buffer pool. This is just an array of Page objects. The buffer manager is used by (the code for) access methods, heap files, and relational operators to read / write /allocate / de-allocate pages. The Buffer Manager makes calls to the underlying DB class object, which actually performs these functions on disk pages. Replacement policies for the buffer manager can be changed easily at compile time.

File Manager:

It keep track of all the files stored on the secondary storage and is responsible for the searching, extracting and presenting the information to the query engine, so the operations to be performed by the query will be operated on the desired data. It uses different structures and indexes to keep track of the files on the storage media. Function of the file manager is to manage disk space for storage and manage data structure used for storing information.

The Main Functions Of file Manager Are: –

• Convert operations in user's Queries coming from the application programs or combination of DML Compiler and Query optimizer which is known as Query Processor from user's logical view to physical file system.

• Controls DBMS information access that is stored on disk.

• It also controls handling buffers in main memory.

• It also enforces constraints to maintain consistency and integrity of the data.

• It also synchronizes the simultaneous operations performed by the concurrent users.

• It also controls the backup and recovery operations.

2.6 <u>ESTIMATED COSTS AND PROGRAM EVALUATION:</u>

<u>One Time Cost :</u>

Analysis	**1,000**
Software development	**3,000**
Computer hardware and supporting system software	**20,000**
Total one-time costs	**24,000**

<u>Annual Operating Costs:</u>

Maintenance	**5,000**
Utilities	**1,000**
Supplies	**1,000**
Yearly backup for system	**1,500**
Total annual operating costs	**8,500**

Activities	Duration (in Person Weeks)
Analysis (T1)	4
Design (T2)	5
Coding (T3)	10
Testing (T4)	3
Final Documentation (T5)	4
Complete Documentation (T6)	5

ANALYSIS

3.1 PROCESS OVERVIEW

Although the analysis phase greatly resembles the Preliminary Investigation phase, any activities previously executed in the preliminary Investigation phase will now be executed in more depth. The completion of the Preliminary Investigation phase narrows the scope of the activities in the Analysis phase so that efforts will focus on the chosen solution. Now the models for the current system and proposed system can be fleshed out with more detailed specifications. Because the steering committee has approved the new system, work can begin in earnest. The Analysis phase has six basic activities:

- Study the existing system.
- Review the conclusions obtained by the preliminary Investigation phase recommended solution, feasibility issues, and rejection of alternative solutions.
- Prepare the model of the new system.
- Revise the preliminary design.
- Devise the detailed schedule for project implementation.
- Prepare the report on the Analysis phase for review by management.

Thus, analysis phase provides the first technical representation of a system. It is easy to understand and maintain. Deals with the problem of size by partitioning the system. Uses graphics whenever possible. Differentiates between essential information versus implementation information. It helps in the tracking and evaluation of interfaces. It provides tools other than narrative text to describe software logic and policy

3.2 SOFTWARE ANALYSIS:

The analysis phase begins when we realize that we have to develop interfaces for the expert and the non-expert users. For the non-expert user we need to provide an area where the user can write the query in natural language and then submit it to the intelligent engine which will process it and transform it to the SQL query and then forward it to the query engine, where the SQL query will be executed and we also have to provide the area where we can display the retrieved data to the user.

For the expert users, as we have already mentioned what are the problems faced by it, we conclude that we have to develop that interface which will enable the expert user to write the queries even without exact knowledge of the syntax of SQL queries. So, in that regard we have decided to design an interface which will have all the options for different queries and the expert user will easily use any query to manipulate the database. Also, we will be presenting the schema description of the database to the user so that it can easily understand the structure of database.

We will be using SQL-server for implementing this enhanced engine concept because SQL-server has got maximum number of operations which are used to operate the database and also the SQL-server is used by many organizations and will be an easy and appropriate way to implement the above discussed concept.

We are using .NET for the implementation of this project, because the .NET Framework offers a number of benefits to developers:

- A consistent programming model
- Direct support for security
- Simplified development efforts
- Easy application deployment and maintenance

3.3 HARDWARE REQUIREMENT

Since the application is based on "THREE TIER ARCHITECTURE", the following hardware is required at:

1. **CLIENT SYSTEM:-**

   1) Processor Pentium III or higher.
   2) 512MB of RAM or more.
   3) 40GB Hard Disk or more.
   4) Network Adapter or Modem.
   5) Monitor.

2. **SERVER SYSTEM: -**

   1.) RAM (at least) 512 MB.
   2.) LAN Card (Speed) 100mbps
   3.) Pentium-IV Processor or Above.
   4.) Hard Disk (80 GB).

3.4 SOFTWARE REQUIRED:

CLIENT SYSTEM:-

- Operating systems: - "WIN-XP" / "WIN-98" / "WIN-2000 SERVER or ADVANCE SERVER" / "WIN-2003 SERVER or ADVANCE SERVER", LINUX etc.
- Web browser: - Internet Explorer, Netscape Navigator, Mozilla, Opera etc.

SERVER SYSTEM: -

- o Operating systems: - "WIN-XP" / "WIN-98" / "WIN-2000 SERVER or ADVANCE SERVER" / "WIN-2003 SERVER or ADVANCE SERVER", LINUX etc.
- Web browser: - internet explorer, Netscape Navigator, Mozilla, Opera etc.
- Internet Information Server (IIS).
- Visual Studio 2010.
- .NET framework 2.0 or higher.
- SQL Server.

3.5 Interface Design

The value interface of a web Application is its "first impression" regardless of the its content, the sophistication of its processing capabilities & services & the overall benefit of web Application itself a poorly designed interface will disappoint the user and may infect cause the user to go elsewhere . Keeping all these consideration in mind we have designed our interface very toughly (and keeping present trend in mind) the interface used by us is menu driven where the heading of menu give user think of its type. So, we need to design an interface that will be attractive and must fulfill the needs of users.

For the implementation of this concept, we use .NET using Visual Studio 2010. Active Server Pages (ASP) is a tool for creating dynamic and interactive web pages. ASP is a Microsoft technology which works by allowing us to use the functionality of a programming language that will generate the HTML for the web page dynamically. ASP was officially announced to the world by Microsoft on July 16th 1996, codenamed

22

Denali. It gained popularity when it was bundled with IIS v3.0 a web server suite in March1997. Now the latest version is IIS 5.0 which comes with Windows2000. An ASP file is just the same as an HTML file. An ASP file can contain text, HTML tags and scripts like VbScript and JavaScript. The scripts are enclosed in tags <%---your code goes here---%>. Scripts in an ASP file are executed on the server. An ASP file has the file extension ".asp".

The .NET Framework represents a unified, object-oriented set of services and libraries that embrace the changing role of new network-centric and network-aware software. In fact, the .NET Framework is the first platform designed from the ground up with the Internet in mind.

When a browser requests an HTML file, the server returns the file. When a browser requests an ASP file, the server calls ASP. ASP reads the ASP file and executes the scripts in the file. Finally, the ASP file is returned to the browser as a plain HTML file.

Allows you to run programs in programming language that are not supported by your browser. Downloading time is less than client side dynamic web technologies such as Java applets. Dynamically edit, change or add any content of a Web page. Response to user queries or data submitted from HTML forms. Access any data or databases and return the results to a browser. The advantages of using ASP instead of CGI and Perl, are those of simplicity and speed. Provides security since your ASP code cannot be viewed from the browser. Since ASP files are returned as plain HTML, they can be viewed in any browser. Clever ASP programming can minimize the network traffic

An ASP file normally contains HTML tags, just as a standard HTML file. In addition, an ASP file can contain **server scripts**, surrounded by the delimiters **<%** and **%>**. Server scripts are **executed on the server,** and can contain any expressions, statements, procedures, or operators that are valid for the scripting language you use.

DESIGN

4.1 OVERVIEW:

The activities in the Design phase are executed in order to furnish the details needed for the coding of the system. The appropriate hardware and software platforms for the system's implementation are selected. These basic issues are depicted in fig. although these issues are listed in the Design phase. They were under consideration throughout the earlier phases. The users also actively participate in the Design Phase by evaluating the analyst's proposals for the user interfaces, such as screen designs and report formats. The format of the computer files is defined in this phase along with the specifications for test data needed for program testing activities in the next phase. The formats for input data and output data are also specified, the medium for the system's inputs and outputs is chosen, and any paper forms form manually recorded data are drafted, Testing procedures are formulated in a preliminary manner.

The training of the users is considered in this phase, although final plans are typically deferred to the implementation phase. The computer programs are described in a detailed fashion, typically by a diagramming technique known as structure charts. After this phase is completed, the details of the system have been fully specified. The system is now ready for programming to begin. Preliminary plans are also drawn up for the installation of the new system; final plans will be produced during the Implementation phase. Before moving into the next phase, the checkpoint occurs: Management decides whether the activities to date have progressed satisfactorily and, if so, approves continuation of the project. Thus this phase involves preliminary or high-level design of the main modules with an overall picture (i.e., a block diagram) and how the parts fit together (i.e., flow chart). The language and the operating system and the hardware components should all be known at this time. Then a detailed or low-level design is created, perhaps with prototyping as proof of the concept or to firm up the requirements. Thus we conclude that the design phase is when we build the plan for how we will we take our project through the rest of the SDL process – from implementation, to verification, to release. Here we design the best practice to follow for this phase by way of functionality and design specifications, and we perform risk analysis to identify threats and vulnerabilities in our software.

The following actions are prohibited:

- Except for security products, disabling of the firewall or changing the state of the firewall. The firewall must only be disabled by explicit user action.
- Any service or feature that adds, changes, or removes firewall rules automatically at runtime. Except at setup time (that is, during the installation process), programs, features, and services that are not designed specifically as firewall management utilities must not change firewall settings unless the user has explicitly initiated some action.
- Any service or feature that allows a port to be opened or a rule to be enabled by a user without administrative privileges. A user must be acting as an administrator in order to change the settings of the firewall, and no service or feature (both Windows and non-Windows) must bypass this restriction.
- Silent activation or enabling of any feature that permits other programs to receive unsolicited traffic. For example, the RemoteAdmin feature permits other RPC-based programs to receive unsolicited traffic. In such cases, the system must obtain user consent before activating such functionality.
- Programs, services, and features may not configure an external device (for example, a NAT gateway) without user consent.
- Any interference with Post Setup Security Update or similar functionality designed to ensure that the system is up-to-date prior to accepting incoming traffic without user consent. Creation of inbound firewall rules unless the feature or service will receive unsolicited inbound traffic.

The following actions are permitted:

- Programs, services, and features may define a firewall rule and leave it disabled for the sake of making it convenient for the user to enable the rule later on. All cryptography must comply with the Microsoft Cryptographic Standards for SDL-covered products. Adhere to the SDL crypto requirements, which at a high-level are: Use AES for symmetric enc/dec.
- Use 128-bit or better symmetric keys. Use RSA for asymmetric enc/dec and signatures. Use 2048-bit or better RSA keys. Use SHA-256 or better for hashing and message-authentication codes. Support certificate revocation. Limit lifetimes for

symmetric keys and asymmetric keys without associated certificates Support cryptographically secure versions of SSL (must not support SSL v2). Use cryptographic certificates reasonably and choose reasonable certificate validity periods. (New for SDL 5.2) Use Transport Layer encryption securely. Properly use Transport Layer Security (TLS) when communicating with another entity, and verify that your service checks the Common Name attribute to be sure it matches the host with which you intended to communicate. Verify that your service consults a certificate revocation list (CRL) for an updated list of revoked certificates at a frequent interval. If your service is accessible via a browser, confirm that no security warnings appear at any visited URL for any supported browser.

4.2 <u>Risk Analysis</u>

During the design phase of development, carefully review security and privacy requirements and expectations to identify security concerns and privacy risks. It is efficient to identify and address these concerns and risks during the design phase For security concerns, threat modeling is a systematic process that is used to identify threats and vulnerabilities in software. You must complete threat modeling during project design. A team cannot build secure software unless it understands the assets the project is trying to protect, the threats and vulnerabilities introduced by the project, and details of how the project will mitigate those threats. Threat modeling applies to all products and services, all code types, and all platforms. Verify that threat models exist for all attack surfaces and new features and each threat model includes: diagrams showing the software and all trust boundaries, STRIDE threats enumerated for each element that crosses a trust boundary or that connects to a data flow that crosses a trust boundary, mitigations for all threats, a list of assumptions made while threat modeling, all non platform external dependencies that the elements in the threat model rely on. Important risk analysis considerations include the following:

Threats and vulnerabilities that exist in the project's environment or that result from interaction with other systems. You cannot consider the design phase complete unless you have a threat model or models that include such considerations. Threat models are critical components of the design phase and reference a project's functional and design specifications to describe vulnerabilities and mitigations. Code that was created by external development groups in either source or object form. It is very important to evaluate carefully any code from sources external to your team. Failure to do so might cause security vulnerabilities about which the project team is unaware. Threat models that include all legacy code if the project is a new release of an existing program. Such code could have been written before much was known about software security, and therefore could contain vulnerabilities.

4.3 <u>METHODOLOGY USED:</u>

The methodology used for developing this system is PROTOTYPING MODEL. We can further understand the working of this process with the help of the figure. We have used this model for developing our project because with a prototyping model we are able to produce the prototypes of our project and help us to examine it and then suggest changes to it, so that more and more requirements will be gathered and we will develop more efficient system. Also in order to develop a system that will process the natural language input we are not sure about the sentences or the queries typed in natural language. So, we must develop a prototype and check its efficiency for some user queries in natural language, and then enhance this prototype to accept more and more user queries in natural language. Thus by making use of this model it has become easy for us to develop such a project which is able to process natural language and provide some more additional functionality to the user as required.

Also, as it is evident from the figure that in prototype model we just make the prototypes in order to clarify the requirements of the user and when the requirements are final we start actual development of the project and are hence able to save time, resources and develop a more user friendly and user oriented system that will be able to provide all the necessary things to interact with any database in a user friendly environment. This model is used here because detailed input, output requirements are not present in the beginning, and thus it is felt that a prototyping model will be more suitable for development. In this model, we will create a quick design and then invite user to test the developed system and refine requirements if any. Thus, the process for development will be iterative.

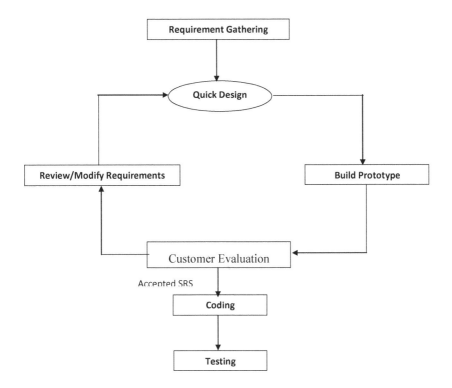

"PROTOTYPING MODEL"

Often, a customer defines a set of general objectives for software but does not identify detailed input, processing or output requirements. In other cases, the developer may be unsure of the efficiency of an algorithm, the adaptability of an operating system, or the form that human/machine interaction should take. In these, and many other situations, a prototyping model offers the best approach.

It generally has the following steps:

1. Requirement Gathering
2. Quick Design
3. Build Prototype
7. Testing

4. Customer Evaluation
5. Review/Modify Requirements
6. Coding

1. Requirement gathering:

In this phase we collect all the requirements needed to develop the project i.e., we collect the information about the hardware and software requirements and list the functionalities of the system which it must possess to accomplish the task. Thus, this step involves understanding the very basics product requirements especially in terms of user interface. The more intricate details of the internal design and external aspects like performance and security can be ignored at this stage.

2. Quick Design:

The initial Prototype is developed in this stage, where the very basic requirements are showcased and user interfaces are provided. These features may not exactly work in the same manner internally in the actual software developed and the workarounds are used to give the same look and feel to the customer in the prototype developed.

3. Build Prototype and Evaluation:

The prototype developed is then presented to the customer and the other important stakeholders in the project. The feedback is collected in an organized manner and used for further enhancements in the product under development.

4. Review & Modification:

The feedback and the review comments are discussed during this stage and some negotiations happen with the customer based on factors like , time and budget constraints and technical feasibility of actual implementation. The changes accepted are again incorporated in the new Prototype developed and the cycle repeats until customer expectations are met.

5. Coding & Testing:

In this phase the actual coding of whole project takes place and finally the testing of that code is performed. At this stage the requirements are finalized and are fully known.

4.4 DATA FLOW DIAGRAMS:

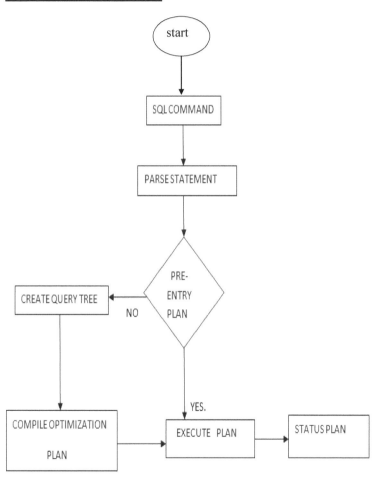

"QUERY EXECUTION PROCESS"

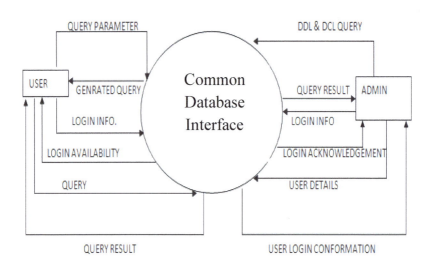

CONTEXT LEVEL DFD.(0.0)

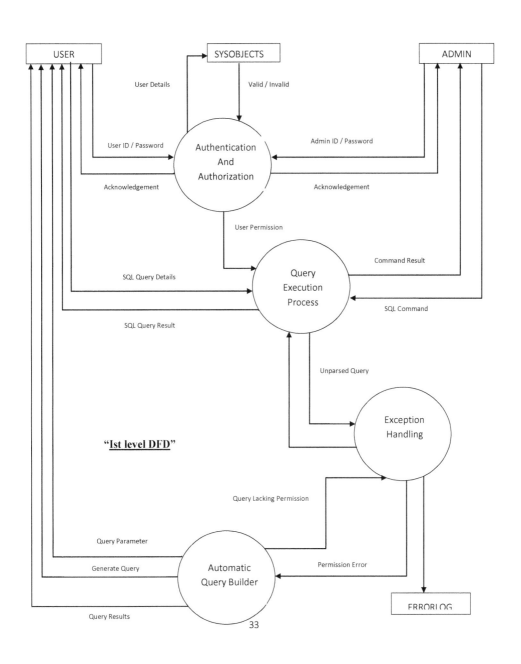

USER

SYSOBJECTS

ADMIN

User Details

Valid / Invalid

User ID / Password

Admin ID / Password

Authentication
And
Authorization

Acknowledgement

Acknowledgement

User Permission

Command Result

SQL Query Details

Query
Execution
Process

SQL Command

SQL Query Result

Unparsed Query

Exception
Handling

"Ist level DFD"

Query Lacking Permission

Query Parameter

Generate Query

Automatic
Query Builder

Permission Error

ERRORLOG

Query Results

33

4.5 <u>TOOLS USED IN THE DEVELOPMENT PROCESS:</u>

1. ASP.NET.

2. HTML.

3. Visual Studio 2010.

4. Internet Information Server (IIS)

5. CSS.

6. Web browser

1. <u>ASP.NET:</u>

ASP.NET is an open source server-side Web application framework designed for Web development to produce dynamic Web pages. It was developed by Microsoft to allow programmers to build dynamic web site, web applications and web services. It was first released in January 2002 with version 1.0 of the .NET Framework, and is the successor to Microsoft's Active Server Pages (ASP) technology. ASP.NET is built on the Common Language Runtime (CLR), allowing programmers to write ASP.NET code using any supported .NET language. The ASP.NET SOAP extension framework allows ASP.NET components to process SOAP messages. ASP.NET is in the process of being re- implemented as a modern and modular web framework, together with other frameworks like Entity Framework.

2. <u>HTML:</u>

A web browser can read HTML files and compose them into visible or audible web pages. The browser does not display the HTML tags, but uses them to interpret the content of the page. HTML describes the structure of a website semantically along with cues for presentation, making it a markup language rather than a programming language. HTML elements form the building blocks of all websites. HTML allows images and objects to be embedded and can be used to create interactive forms. It provides a means to create structured documents by denoting structural semantics for text such as headings, paragraphs, lists, links, quotes and other items. It can embed scripts written in languages such as JavaScript which affect the behavior of HTML web pages. Web browsers can also refer to Cascading Style Sheets (CSS) to define the look and layout of text and other material. The W3C, maintainer of both the HTML and the CSS standards, encourages the use of CSS over explicit presentational HTML.

3. **Visual studio 2010:**

Microsoft Visual Studio is an integrated development environment (IDE) from Microsoft. It is used to develop computer programs for Microsoft Windows super-family of operating systems, as well as web sites, web applications and web services. Visual Studio uses Microsoft software development platforms such as Windows API, Windows Forms, Windows Presentation Foundation, Windows Store and Microsoft Silverlight. It can produce both native code and managed code. Visual Studio includes a code editor supporting IntelliSense as well as code refactoring. The integrated debugger works both as a source- level debugger and a machine-level debugger. Other built-in tools include a forms designer for building GUI applications, web designer, class designer, and database schema designer. It accepts plug-ins that enhance the functionality at almost every level—including adding support for source-control systems (like Subversion) and adding new toolsets like editors and visual designers for domain-specific languages or toolsets for other aspects of the software development lifecycle (like the Team Foundation Server client: Team Explorer). Visual Studio supports different programming languages and allows the code editor and debugger to support (to varying degrees) nearly any programming language, provided a language-specific service exists. Built-in languages include C, C++ and C++/CLI (via Visual C++), VB.NET (via Visual Basic .NET), C# (via Visual C#), and F# (as of Visual Studio 2010). Support for other languages such as M, Python, and Ruby among others is available via language services installed separately. It also supports XML/XSLT, HTML / XHTML, JavaScript and CSS.

4. **Internet Information Server (IIS):**

Internet Information Services (IIS, formerly Internet Information Server) is an extensible web server created by Microsoft for use with Windows NT family. IIS supports HTTP, HTTPS, FTP, FTPS, SMTP and NNTP. It has been an integral part of the Windows NT family since Windows NT 4.0, though it may be absent from some editions (e.g. Windows XP Home edition). IIS is not turned on by default when Windows is installed. The IIS Manager is accessed through the Microsoft Management Console or Administrative Tools in the Control Panel.

5. CSS:

Cascading Style Sheets (CSS) is a style sheet language used for describing the look and formatting of a document written in a markup language. While most often used to style web pages and user interfaces written in HTML and XHTML, the language can be applied to any kind of XML document, including plain XML, SVG and XUL. CSS is a cornerstone specification of the web and almost all web pages use CSS style sheets to describe their presentation. CSS is designed primarily to enable the separation of document content from document presentation, including elements such as the layout, colors, and fonts. This separation can improve content accessibility , provide more flexibility and control in the specification of presentation characteristics, enable multiple pages to share formatting, and reduce complexity and repetition in the structural content (such as by allowing for table-less web design). CSS can also allow the same markup page to be presented in different styles for different rendering methods, such as on-screen, in print, by voice (when read out by a speech-based browser or screen reader) and on Braille- based , tactile devices. It can also be used to allow the web page to display differently depending on the screen size or device on which it is being viewed. While the author of a document typically links that document to a CSS file, readers can use a different style sheet, perhaps one on their own computer, to override the one the author has specified. However if the author or the reader did not link the document to a specific style sheet the default style of the browser will be applied. CSS specifies a priority scheme to determine which style rules apply if more than one rule matches against a particular element. In this so called cascade, priorities or weights are calculated and assigned to rules, so that the results are predictable.

Chapter - 4

IMPLEMENTATION

6.1 Overview:

6.2 Natural Language Query Processing Interface

6.3 SQL Query Interface

6.4 Schema Description Interface

6.5 Manage User Interface

6.6 Log-in Interface

6.1 Overview:

In order to implement this project we have developed following files:

1. Natural language processing interface:
   - Nlq.aspx
   - Nlq.aspx.cs
2. SQL query interface:
   - Sqlquery.aspx
   - Sqlquery.aspx.cs
3. Schema description interface:
   - Objectbrowser.aspx
   - Objectbrowser.aspx.cs
4. Manage user interface:
   - Manageuser.aspx
   - Manageuser.aspx.cs
5. Login interface:
   - Login.aspx
   - Login.aspx.cs

Also the common code used by all the above CS files is written in a class file with name "myclass.cs". Also the master page is designed with name "mymaster.master". We have also designed a home page for our project which will inform the user about the system and will provide it the access to all the interfaces.

Apart from this we have used many "CSS" and "java-script" files which are used to design the interfaces. We have used CSS for formatting the HTML document because it provides an easy way to format it and has got different in-built procedures for formatting. Java-script is a client side programming language which will execute the code embedded in the HTML file at the client side and hence making the system more efficient in response.

The different modules and their implementation is discussed in detail as:

6.2 <u>NATURAL LANGUAGE QUERY PROCESSING INTERFACE</u>

This interface forms the heart of our project because this interface is responsible for taking the queries in a natural language (English) as input, processes them and then is able to execute them to provide the desired result to the user. This interface is designed in such a way that here the user can only retrieve the information from the pre-defines databases and is not able to modify the structure of the database or any table, this is because, this interface is only meant for those database users who don't have got the prior knowledge about the SQL and these users only want to retrieve the information from already created databases and tables. So, we can say this interface is responsible for performing/executing the "select" queries.

The major challenge with this interface is that the user can provide sufficient or in sufficient information for the transformation of user query into the SQL query. So, the system has to check for the sufficient information during the processing of the natural language queries and inform the user about the insufficient information typed by him/her. The another challenge is that the user can also type the names of attributes, tables and databases with wrong spelling, here the system checks each and every word in the typed query and matches it with the information in the meta-data of database, if it is matches (with some threshold distance between two strings) then that correct table name or the database name is substituted in the actual SQL query which is to be formulated thus by this way the system has become robust. The checking of the valid and correct names of tables and attributes is done by following pseudo code:

Thus, by using the above pseudo code we are able to get the names of the tables and the attributes, that too correct names, for the query to be formulated. Also the system must check for the "minimum" or "maximum" etc words in the user query and then must act accordingly on those queries. To check them following procedure is used:

39

So if this flag is set then the query will be formulated in different way, according to the query for the keyword and finally the desired result is achieved.

We also have to eliminate the unwanted tokens from the user query in order to reduce the computation time and only use that part of user query that is necessary for the formulation of correct query. These unwanted words are called stop-words and can be eliminated by following procedure:

So, this will provide us with those tokens in the user query which are sufficient to formulate the desired correct SQL query.

Our enhanced engine is also responsible for identifying the conjunctive clause in the user query, which is in a natural language. By this way we get an idea whether the query has the condition part or not. These conjunctive words are identified by following way:

Once all these things are done, we are able to get the names of tables and the names of the attributes which the user wants from the system to fetch from the database, and also we will get the different parameters which will support in the formulation of the SQL query. Then using all these things we are able to formulate the SQL query, which is then executed by the query engine and provides the desired result to the user for his/her natural language query.

Thus, the summarization of all the above procedure is given using an example as:

QUERY ENTERED BY THE USER:

show me the names of suppliers with rating greater than 4

USEFULL TOKENS EXTRACTED BY THE ENHANCED ENGINE:

show, names, suppliers, with, rating, greater, 4,

FIELDS RETREIVED:

name, rating

TABLES RETREIVED :

supplier

QUERY FORMULATED :

select a.name, a.rating from supplier as a where a.rating >4

Thus, finally this formulated query is given to the traditional query engine for execution and after execution the results are presented to the user. If the user's natural language query does not contain enough information for the formulation of the SQL query, then the system informs the user about it and asks it to re-type its query with sufficient and proper information and if the information is sufficient and the this enhanced engine is able to transform it into a SQL query, then the process continues with the SQL query generation and finally executes it.

6.3 <u>SQL QUERY INTERFACE</u>

We have designed this interface for the expert user only i.e., the user who has the prior knowledge of SQL and can easily understand different operations performed with the database. This interface provides the user with all the commonly user SQL queries whose syntax is a bit difficult to remember. Our enhanced engine also enables the user to type the SQL queries directly also. Thus the user can also execute those queries which are not pre-defined in our system. To work in this interface the user first selects a database and then a table from that selected database and then the user gets the access to the different options available in this interface.

So, in this interface we initially present to the user with the list of different databases in the system using a dynamic grid-view control, where from the user can select any database whose tables are presented in another grid-view control. The user then selects one of the tables from the list and then gets the access to the options in this interface, which it can use for the execution of different operations on the database. This interface also provides a list of all the attributes and their data-types of a particular table to the user. Using this information user can easily decide whether to use quotes or not when an insertion operation is performed. The different operations a user can perform automatically with this interface are given as:

1. Retrieve whole table content.
2. Retrieve particular table content.
3. Insert values to the table.
4. Update the table content.

5. Delete the table content.
6. Create a new table.
7. Create a new database.
8. Create a view of table.
9. Delete a column of table.
10. Modify the structure of table.
11. Delete a entire table.

Here we have used many buttons to select one of the many operations, which when selected generates the SQL query for that operation in the textbox and then the user modifies this generated query (if needed) and finally clicks the execute button to execute the query. After execution of the query which is in the textbox the result is shown to the user again using the grid-view control or by a message. If on executing the query generated an error occurs then that is also reported to the users using an error message. The working of this interface can be clearly explained using the blow given example:

Suppose in a list of databases the database "university" is present and suppose the user selects it. When the user selects the "university" database, a list of all tables in this database is presented to the user. Suppose the user selects a table with name "student" from the list. After this the user gets access to all the controls in the system. Suppose the user clicks on the "insert values to table" button, then the query to insert values to this table will be automatically generate in the textbox as:

Insert into student

(name,roll_number,registration_number,d_o_b,semister,date_of_admission,District,state,na tionality,phone_number) values

(value1,value2,value3,value4,value5,value6,value7,value8,value9,value10)

Thus, as show above these attribute names are generated automatically, the user only has to select a database and then the table in it, rest the names of all the attributes will be generated automatically by the system. The user will then write the corresponding values at the "value1", "value2" etc and use quotes where needed using the list of data-types against each data-type and finally when all the appropriate values are written then the user will press "execute" button to execute this query. Then if the query is successfully executed then a message generated by the system will depict it.

Thus, in the similar way all other options can generate different SQL queries and the user can use them to interact with the database in a very user friendly manner, without the need to remember the syntax of different SQL queries and names of all the databases, tables and the attributes of tables. Thus it forms an easy interface for the expert database user to interact with the database and perform different database operation easily and efficiently.

6.4 SCHEMA DESCRIPTION INTERFACE

This interface provides a list of all the attributes in a table with the data-type of each attribute and informs whether the attribute can have null value or not, to the database user. This interface also provides user with the ability to edit or delete or add any attribute to the table selected. Here again the user is provided with the list of databases and the selection of which provides with the list of tables, among which one can be selected to show and modify its attributes.

To add new column/attribute to the selected table the user only has to click the "add" button and write the details of this new attribute and then click on "save" button, for this we make use of following SQL query:

alter table " + Session["tablename"].ToString() + " add " + txtcname.Text + " " + dtype + " " + setnull

Here, *Session["tablename"].tostring()* gives the table selected by the user, which we have saved as a session variable with name "tablename". *Txtname.text* gives name of new attribute whose data-type is saved in the variable *dtype* and whether to accept null value or not is saved in a Boolean variable *setnull.*

To delete a column user just have to click the delete button against each column name and then click save button. The SQL query used here is:

alter table " + Session["tablename"].ToString() + " drop column " + e.CommandArgument.ToString()

43

Here, *e.CommandArgument.ToString()* gives the name of the column selected for deletion operation.

Similarly, to edit a column user must click on the edit button, by which an edit label will be visible against each column. The user then clicks one of the label and the corresponding column can be edited (i.e., we can change the data-type or nullable value of the column). The SQL query used here is:

alter table " + Session["tablename"].ToString() + " alter column " + t1.Text + " " + newtype + " " + setnull

Here again t1 contains the attribute name, newtype contains the new data-type for the attribute, and the setnull specifies whether to allow null values to this attribute or not. This query will be executed only when the user will click on the save button. Also when the changes will be made to the attribute it will be immediately evident on the screen once we click the save button.

6.5 MANAGE USER INTERFACE

This interface is designed to provide the easy way to the user for managing the database users. This interface enables the database administrator to easily create the user for the database and assign a particular database to it i.e., a default database for this particular user. This interface also provides a list of all the existing database users, the administrator can select one among them and then click the delete-button to delete that particular database user. With this interface we can create either a database administrator or a simple database user. For the database users we can enforce the password policy and the password expiration by just selecting these options in the interface for the user created.

The SQL query used to create a database administrator is given as:

"create login ["+txtname.Text +"] from windows with default_database = ["+DropDownList1.SelectedValue +"]"

Here *txtname.Text* contains the database administrator-name, the default database is selected from the drop-down menu which contains the list of all the databases in the system.

Similarly, to create a simple database user we have used the following SQL query in our interface:

"create login [" + txtname.Text + "] with password='" + txtpwd.Text + "',
default_database=[" + DropDownList1.SelectedValue + "], check_expiration=" + pwdexp
+ " ,check_policy=" + pwdplcy

Here *txtname.Text* contains the database user-name with password in *txtpwd.Text*, the default database is selected from the drop-down menu which contains the list of all the databases in the system, for the enforcing the password expiration and the password policy we use two Boolean variables *pwdexp* and *pwdplcy* respectively.

Both these Queries will be executed only when the user (i.e., database administrator) will click the create-button. After creating the new user it will be appended to the list in this interface.

   To delete the existing database user, the administrator only have to select the existing user and click on the delete-button, due to which the following query will be executed:

"drop login[" + ddlusers.SelectedValue + "]"

This will delete the database user selected from the list, and after ckicking the delete-button this user will be deleted and will not be present in the list next-time.

6.6 LOG-IN INTERFACE

This interface allows the user to enter the following details:

1. Location of data-source.
2. Name of data-source.
3. Authentication type.
4. User-name.
5. Password.

This interface collects the above information about the particular user and verifies the authentication of this user with the database server. If this user is authenticated user of database then it allows the user to access the system, otherwise an error message is displayed to the user.

When the administrator logs-in following code is used:

Session["auth"] = "admin";

OleDbConnection con = new OleDbConnection();

con.ConnectionString = "provider=sqloledb.1; data source=" + ds.Text + "; initial
catalog=master; integrated Security=sspi";

```
con.Open();
Response.Redirect("home.aspx");
```

And when the simple database user logs-in, the following code is used:

```
Session["auth"] = "";
Session["uname"] = uname.Text;
Session["password"] = pwd.Text;
OleDbConnection con = new OleDbConnection();
con.ConnectionString = " provider=sqloledb.1; data source=" + ds.Text + "; initial
catalog=master;user id=" + uname.Text + "; password=" + pwd.Text;
con.Open();
Response.Redirect("home.aspx");
```

If any exception occurs during the execution of above code, then an error message will be displayed to the user, with the help of which the user can then type the correct information in the given fields.

Also we have created a log-out page which when accessed by the user will delete all the session variables for that session using *session.abandon* command and will redirect the control of user to the log-in page for another user to log-in to the system.

All these above sections will completely implement our project and will provide all the necessary functionality to the system, which the user can use to interact with the database in a very easy, efficient and secure way.

Also the databases used for implementing our project will be constructed in such a way that the names of the tables and their attributes will be those which are used in real life, .for-example in a university database the table name should be student, teachers, etc and their attributes will be name, id, address, phone-number etc (i.e., names which we use in real life). Only then we will be able to efficiently deal with the natural language processing of the user queries, because the user will also use these real-life names of tables, databases and the attributes of tables.

Chapter - 7

SOFTWARE TESTING

7.1 Overview

7.1.1 Goals & Objectives:

7.1.2 Statement of Scope:

7.1.3 Testing Principles:

7.1.4 Test Case:

7.2 Testing Process

7.3 Testing Approaches Used In Our Project

7.1 OVERVIEW:

Software testing is a critical element of the ultimate review of specification design and coding. Testing of software leads to the uncovering of errors in the software functional and performance requirements are met. Testing also provides a good indication of software reliability and software quality as a whole. The result of different phases of testing are evaluated and then compared with the expected results. If the errors are uncovered they are debugged and corrected. A strategy approach to software testing has the generic characteristics: Testing begins at the module level and works "outwards" towards the integration of the entire computer based system. Different testing techniques are appropriate at different points of time. Testing and debugging are different activities, but debugging must be accommodated in the testing strategy.

7.1.1 Goals & Objectives:

Testing is a process of executing a program with the intent of finding an error. A good test case is one that has a probability of finding an as yet undiscovered error. A successful test is one that uncovers an as yet undiscovered error. Our Objective is to design test processes that systematically uncover different classes of errors and do so with minimum amount of time and effort.

7.1.2 Statement of Scope:

A description of the scope of the software testing is developed. All the features to be tested are noted. The basic principles that guides software testing are:

1. All test cases should be traceable top customer requirements. The most severe defects from the customer's point of view are those that cause the program to fail to meet its requirements.

2. Test case should be planned long before testing begins. Testing plan can begin as soon as the requirement model is complete. Detailed definition of the test cases can begin as soon as the design is solidified. Therefore, the entire test can be planned before any code has been generated.

3. Testing should begin "in the small" and progress towards "in the large". The first test planned and executed generally focus on the individual modules. As testing progresses testing shifts focus in an attempt to find errors in integrating clusters of modules and ultimately in the entire system.

7.1.3 Testing Principles:

The basic principles that guide software testing are: -

1. All test cases should be traceable top customer requirements. The most severe defects from the customer's point of view are those that cause the program to fail to meet its requirements.

2. Test case should be planned long before testing begins. Testing plan can begin as soon as the requirement model is complete. Detailed definition of the test cases can begin as soon as the design is solidified. Therefore all the test can be planned before any code has been generated.

3. The Pareto principle applies to software testing. Stated simply the Pareto principle implies that 80% of all errors uncovered during testing will likely to be traceable to 20% of all program modules. The program of course is to isolate these suspect modules and to thoroughly test them.

4. Testing should begin "in the small" and progress towards "in the large". The first test planned and executed generally focus on the individual modules. As testing progresses testing shifts focus in an attempt to find errors in integrating clusters of modules and ultimately in the entire system.

5. Exhaustive testing is not possible. The number of paths permutations for even a moderately sized program is exceptionally large. For this reason it is impossible to execute every combination of path during testing. It is possible however to ensure that all conditions in the procedural design have been exercise To be most effective an independent third party should conduct testing. The third party has the highest probability of finding the errors.

7.1.4 Test Case:

Before the project is released, it has to has pass through a test cases suit, so that the required functionality is met and previous functionality of the system is also not broken to do this, there is an existing test cases which checks for the previous functionality. New test cases are prepared and added to this existing test suit to check for the added functionality.

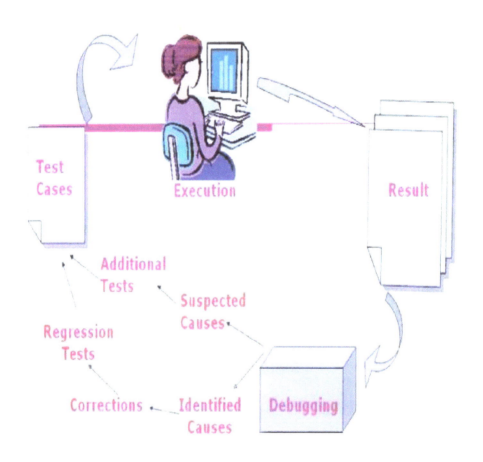

"A pictorial representation of software testing"

7.2 <u>TESTING PROCESS:</u>

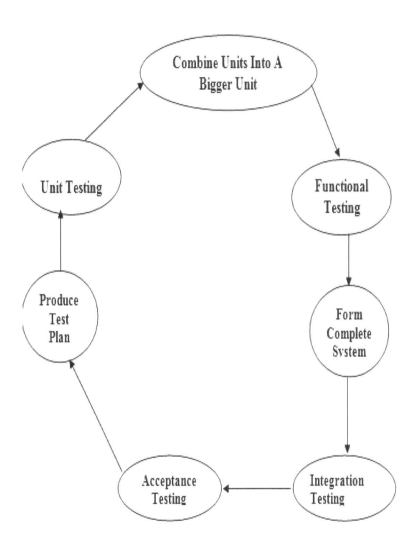

7.3 TESTING APPROACHES USED IN OUR PROJECT:

The module interface is tested to ensure that information properly flows into and out of the program unit under test. The unit testing is normally considered as an adjunct step to coding step. Because modules are not a standalone program, drivers and/or stubs software must be developed for each unit. A driver is nothing more than a "main program" that accepts test cases data and passes it to the module. A stub serves to replace the modules that are subordinate to the modules to be tested. A stub may do minimal data manipulation, prints verification of entry and returns.

7.3.1 Black box testing:

Black-box testing is a method of software testing that tests the functionality of an application as opposed to its internal structures or workings. Specific knowledge of the application's code/internal structure and programming knowledge in general is not required. Test cases are built around specifications and requirements, i.e., what the application is supposed to do. It uses external descriptions of the software, including specifications, requirements, and designs to derive test cases. These tests can be functional or non-functional, though usually functional. The test designer selects valid and invalid inputs and determines the correct output. There is no knowledge of the test object's internal structure.

This method of test can be applied to all levels of software testing:

unit, integration, functional, system and acceptance. It typically comprises most if not all testing at higher levels, but can also dominate unit testing as well.

Unit Testing:

In computer programming, unit testing is a software testing method by which individual units of source code, sets of one or more computer program modules together with associated control data, usage procedures, and operating procedures are tested to determine if they are fit for use. Intuitively, one can view a unit as the smallest testable part of an application. In procedural programming, a unit could be an entire module, but it is more commonly an individual function or procedure. In object-oriented programming, a unit is often an entire interface, such as a class, but could be an individual method. Unit tests are short code fragments created by programmers or occasionally by white box testers during the development process. Ideally, each test case is independent from the others. Substitutes such as method stubs, mock objects, fakes, and test harnesses can be used to assist testing a module in isolation. Unit tests are typically written and run by software developers to ensure that code meets its design and behaves as intended.

Functional Test:

Each part of the code was tested individually and the panels were tested individually on all platforms to see if they are working properly.

Performance Test:

These determined the amount of execution time spent on various parts of units and the resulting throughput, response time given by the module

Stress Test:

A lot of test files were made to work at the same time in order to check how much workloads can the unit bear

Structure Test:

These tests were made to check the internal logic of the program and traversing particular execution paths.

Integration Test:

"If they all work individually, they should work when we put them together." The problem of course is "putting them together". This can be done in two ways:

Top down Integration:

Modules are integrated by moving downwards through the control hierarchy, beginning with main control module are incorporated into the structure in either a depth first or breadth first manner.

Bottom up Integration:

It begins with construction and testing with atomic modules i.e. modules at the lowest level of the program structure. Because modules are integrated from the bottom up, processing required for the modules subordinate to a given level is always available and the need of stubs is eliminated.

White-box testing

White-box testing (also known as clear box testing, glass box testing, and transparent box testing and structural testing) is a method of testing software that tests internal structures or workings of an application, as opposed to its functionality. In white-box testing an internal perspective of the system, as well as programming skills, are required and used to design test cases. The tester chooses inputs to exercise paths through the code and determine the appropriate outputs. This is analogous to testing nodes in a circuit, e.g. in-circuit testing (ICT).While white-box testing can be applied at the unit, integration and system levels of the software testing process, it is usually done at the unit level. It can test paths within a unit, paths between units during integration, and between subsystems during a system level test. Though this method of test design can uncover many errors or problems, it might not detect unimplemented parts of the specification or missing requirements.

White-box test design techniques include:

- Control flow testing
- Data flow testing
- Branch testing.
- Path testing.

Chapter-8

CONCLUSION &FUTURE

8.1 Conclusion

8.2 Future Scope

8.1 <u>CONCLUSION</u>:

In this project, we have proposed an easy and unique way to interact with a database, which is not only helpful to a non-expert user but also to an expert user, by providing a user friendly environment and have used the concept of natural language processing to process the user queries typed in natural language like English.

In the early procedures, a user can only interact with database when it has a complete knowledge of SQL (Structured Query Language), because SQL is an ANSI standard for accessing and manipulating the information stored in relational databases, but our proposed interface provides access to any database without the prior knowledge of SQL.

We have also concluded that a non-expert user will have to only retrieve the data from the pre-defined databases, so we have allowed him to retrieve the desired output by typing the queries in natural language (like English) and we have proposed a new procedure to process these natural language queries and convert them to SQL queries for execution. Our proposed system to process natural language queries is so efficient that it can also detect the wrong input and fetches the sufficient information from wrong input, so that it can transform it to the correct data by using meta-data of databases. Thus, this supports the Robustness of our proposed system.

For the expert user we have been able to develop the interface which releases him from the burden of remembering the commonly used SQL queries and their syntax. Our project has provided a user-friendly way to the expert user for accessing and fetching different databases, their tables, attributes and the values with just few clicks. In traditional approach it is a bit difficult task to access the meta-data of stored databases and hence providing an additional information to the user. With our enhanced engine user can easily perform the same task with much ease and minimum effort. Creating new user and deleting an existing user was again a hectic task for a user to deal with. With our proposed system we can maintain the integrity and security of our databases by simply creating or deleting the user. Besides this our proposed system has succeeded in providing controlled access to databases by providing different privilege to different users with ease.

8.2 **FUTURE SCOPE:**

As we have already mentioned that we have provided a natural language access to a user for only retrieving data of pre-defined databases only. In future we can work on this system and increase its efficiency by not only retrieving the data of databases but also providing other relational database operations to be performed using the concept of natural language processing i.e., allowing user to type other queries that will not only retrieve data but also will modify or create databases using natural language (English). These other operations include the operations used to create a database, to modify the existing structure of databases, to insert values to tables of particular database, to update the contents of database or tables of database and to delete the table entries or tables or entire databases. Then we can succeed in making this system a fully natural language processing system which will then relieve the users from comprehending the syntax of various SQL queries and thus making it a completely SQL independent engine to process various queries in natural language.

Chapter-9

BIBLIOGRAPHY

REFERENCES:

[1]Complete Reference .NET (Herbert Schildt).

[2] ASP.NET - Wrox pub (Zab Shelton).

[3] Complete NET unleashed (Pavl. R. Alum).

[4] Html Complete Reference (Laura lemay/ Thomas Powell).

[5] SQL Complete Reference (Julie C. Meloni).

[6] The Internet Complete Ref. (Margaret Levine Young).

[7] .NET programming (Grant Palmer).

WEBSITES:

[1] *http://www.microsoft.com*

[2] *http://www.msdn.com.*

[3] *http://www.dotnetspider.com*

[4] https://www.msdn.microsoft.com/

[5] https://www.tutorialspoint.com/

[6] https://www.microsoftvirtualacademy.com/

[7] https://www.coursera.org/

www.ingramcontent.com/pod-product-compliance
Lightning Source LLC
Chambersburg PA
CBHW041153050326

40690CB00001B/455